# Pieces of Her Mind

## Women Find Their Voice
## in Centuries-Old Forms

3/25/13

Linda –
for my very
dearest friend.
I hope you enjoy
this.
Love,
Connie

*Omega Publications, Palm Springs, CA*

*ISBN: 978-0-9850350-6-8*

*Edited by*
*Alvin Thomas Ethington*

*Page Layout by*
*Omega Publications, Palm Springs, CA*

*www.omegapublications.net*
*Printed in the United States of America*

# List of Graphics and Copyright

Note:

One may wonder why we chose a dragon, a Chinese symbol, for the back cover. One needs to see the *haiga* as a whole; note the poem. What the Japanese did centuries ago with Chinese poetry and art – adapt them and make them their own – we, the women authors of this anthology, are doing with *senryu*, *kyoka* and *haiga* – adapting them and making them our own, thus pulling the tail of the dragon.

.

# Dedication

*for all women*
*who love to learn*
*and speak their minds*

*and*

*for all men*
*who love to learn*
*how our minds think*

# Pieces of Her Mind

## Women Find Their Voice
## in Centuries-Old Forms

# Endorsements

Thank goodness for this anthology. There lies, within this astounding volume, an affirmation of *senryu*'s power, grace, charm, flexibility and vitality. As an editor, I have occasionally allowed myself to fall into the seemingly endless and often somewhat thorny debate concerning the status of *senryu* as a singular form. With this genuinely absorbing collection of poems and essays, we have, at last, a substantial and authoritative answer to those who may question the form's significance. We should have learned by now that the most tangled of dilemmas is best unraveled by the women of this world, and, certainly in the case of this anthology, with such admirable sensitivity and precision. I'm more deeply in love with *senryu* now than I've ever been. — **Liam Wilkinson, Former Editor,** *Prune Juice.*

Whimsy and wisdom. Beauty in structure and form. Feels good. Clever witty women. Ancient and modern. Courage and candor. Touches soul and tickles it.

*Pieces of Her Mind* penetrates the heart of the everyday experience of being a woman going through the passages of life in our modern world — making us laugh, awakening admiration for the elegance of ancient Japan's poetic forms, inspiring us to reveal ourselves with abandon. Like a woman, this book is an artful treasure that can truly be called a modern classic, aesthetically pleasing and emotionally rousing — educating us, enlightening and entertaining us, all at the same time. Already I am learning. I love this book. — **Dianne Collins, Award-winning author of** *Do You QuantumThink? New Thinking That Will Rock Your World.*

# Endorsements

*Senryu* are short aftertastes like amuse-gueule, or small arms visual gunfire, and potent as longer satirical poems. The examples in this book create shredded shooting gallery targets within the bull's-eye area, and will help re-invigorate *senryu* and give a boost to the confidence of new and established writers alike.

The book's bittersweet, ironic, poignant, truthful, and painfully revealing verses will delight the taste buds of readers, as I tend to think honesty has a higher register in *senryu*, if well done. Even if we don't want to see the honesty of *senryu* verse, it's there as checks and balances in our own lives: It feeds a need of a different place than *haiku* can accomplish. — **Alan Summers, *Japan Times* award-winning writer; Editor, *Notes From the Gean*.**

*Pieces of Her Mind* is at turns thought-provoking, creative, charming, and page-turning. I'm amazed at what these eighteen women have done with classical Japanese poetic forms and am both encouraged to try  my hand at writing such poetry myself (the forms are so appealing and spare), and humbled at their skill. — **Jennifer Lawler, award-winning author of the Dojo Wisdom series.**

A well-crafted collection of English language Japanese short form poetry! Through their collaborative learning, hard work, and practically nuanced approach to *senryu, kyoka,* and *haiga*, the women authors of this anthology successfully adapted these centuries-old forms and made them their own. The reader will experience their unique poetic voices in the book. — **Chen-ou Liu, haiku columnist and author of three books.**

# Endorsements

The women who contributed to this work, *Pieces of Her Mind*, have incredible voices. They expressed their passion, humor, strength, and wisdom through an art form which allowed them to discover and expose themselves. My favorite chapters are the ones on laughter and friendship, although I sighed, laughed, and nodded in affirmation throughout the book. I highly recommend this book to anyone who enjoys re-charging her or his sensibilities in moments of time. — **Janie Sullivan, Director, Center for Writing Excellence.**

The collection of *senryu*, *haiga* and *kyoka* in *Pieces of Her Mind* hints at the possibility that these writers may have burned a bra or two while finding their way in an evolving society. Beyond their observant — and often irreverent — approach to life, is a true collaboration of bright, creative and talented women. Each voice is strong and unique. Each voice reflects a distinct vision that colors each writer's world. And yet, this is more than a series of soloists stepping up to the microphone. Together they explore the subjects that make us human: beauty, enlightenment, laughter, passion, strength, truth, wisdom and friendship. The harmonies they create within this framework are genuine and satisfying. And, as is true of all fine writing, we feel less alone having read their words. And besides, what are a few burned bras between friends? — **Deborah Barbour Lundy, published poet of short Japanese poetic forms.**

A thoroughly enjoyable and unexpectedly entertaining volume of verse. Who would've known that ancient forms brought to life by modern writers would yield such an abundance of wit, wisdom, and wordplay? — **Dr Mardy Grothe, author of *Oxymoronica* and *I Never Metaphor I Didn't Like.***

# Table of Contents

# Introduction

## by
## Susan Campion

In September, 2011, a seed was planted by Alvin Thomas Ethington, a published poet and constructivist teacher of a class on short Japanese poetic forms: "I'd like to see a book of *senryu* written by contemporary women." I was intrigued and motivated. After some research, I could not find such a book published. In fact, my research showed that *senryu* originated with men in Japan, dating back to 1746, and was largely dominated by men for years.

Hiroaki Sato (2003) points out: "If the period of two-hundred-and-fifty years since the *senryu* was established as a genre were to be divided into five ages, this would be the fifth." Women writers, such as Alexis Rotella, former President of the *Haiku Society of America*, author of multiple published *senryu* works, and former editor of *Prune Juice* are the forerunners. We women hope to join them and help to describe this content and these forms in new ways. This endeavor is still new. As the pioneering Japanese poet, Inoue Nobuko, (Sako, 2003) said: "women *senryu* writers are still fewer than the stars at daybreak."

I invited a diverse group of seventeen women writers whose work I respected to join me in a learning community to explore both content and form. The content—how do we, as contemporary women—talk about being women with a new voice? The form? Three centuries-old and respected Japanese forms that incorporate satire and irony.

These women live all over the world. They are diverse in age, ethnicity, geographical locations, and experience in writing. Several have been published in online journals as well as in poetry anthologies, and others appreciate the idea of being published at last.

These women all brought different talents and perspectives to the table. Some are recognized editors; others are professional graphic illustrators; others are accomplished in the marketing field.

Despite and because of the diversity in our group, we share some things in common: we are women, committed writers all, who love to learn and to express our opinions.

During the past year, we attended a variety of classes, researched the internet extensively, and joined blogs. We participated in multiple group e-mails and conference calls. We edited each other's work, challenged each other to meet high expectations, and reached consensus on most aspects of this book, a rather amazing feat.

As English Language poets, we enjoyed the study of Japanese Aesthetics and have chosen to honor Japanese influences and aesthetics in our submissions, even to the point of reducing the number of chapters to eight, as eight is a lucky Japanese number.

The result of our mutual learning is this book, which we humbly and proudly share with you.

Special thanks are extended to Alvin Thomas Ethington, who worked tirelessly with the authors to edit and select poems that fit our 'descriptions' of the three short Japanese poetic forms we used. Another big thank you goes to Rama Devi Nina Marshall, who worked with authors and edited all prose pieces. Kudos to Suzanne Fuller, the talent and genius behind the graphic illustrations in this book. And to Robyn Corum and Melissa Bickel who worked untiringly on marketing ideas, we extend our gratitude as well.

## Organization of the Book

This book is organized in eight chapters. The character for the number eight in Japanese is two strokes wider at the bottom to signify a better time or better things to come. Each of these chapters is introduced by the Japanese symbol for the main heading of the chapter. The subtitles of the chapters were agreed upon by the authors.

Within each chapter, the first section consists of *senryu* poems. Following the *senryu* poems is a *haiga*. After the *haiga* are *kyoka* poems. Following the *kyoka* poems are Personal Reflective Essays by the authors that mirror the essence of the chapter's title and the journey of the women contributors on their writing paths.

All poems are organized randomly by author within the chapters and there is also an Index of Authors' Works at the end of the book.

Finally, we share selected resources and references we have discovered during our learning process and invite you to enjoy them as well.

# Prologue

by
Alvin Thomas Ethington

In September of 2011, I approached my online *senryu* class with trepidation. It was the least subscribed of my classes and I had not published at that time in the field. The scholarly world was awash with debates about whether *senryu* was even a separate form from *haiku*.

I had my own ideas, of course. I thought *senryu* was indeed a separate form from *haiku*, as it had arisen independently. I knew from teaching newcomers to Japanese poetry that I would need to concentrate on direct observation and the use of concrete imagery — elements the English-speaking scholarly world concentrating on short Japanese poetic forms assumed all too often. I still hold to these ideas.

My *senryu* class had only three women in it. Much to my surprise, I found something amazing happening. There was a voice I had never heard emerging. It was forged from women's experiences and reminded me of conversations I heard as a child from my mother, aunts, and sisters in a strong women's culture of the American South and Southwest. It reminded me of feminist conversations I heard in the late seventies of the last century at Oberlin College. Combined with those two were whispers of the radical lesbians I knew at Yale, although none of the women in my class was lesbian, and the feminine women's rights culture of California. However, this was a unique voice — brave, but not confrontational; humorous, but not offensive and even sometimes self-deprecatory. It was radical social commentary but phrased in a way all could hear. I thought I had found something new — it was even beyond postmodern in that it created a new COMMUNITY identity.

I am now excited and pleased to see that excitement was well founded as the students in this class, who are contributors to this book, have been accepted for publication elsewhere. Many of the poems found in this book have been published in the online *senryu*, *kyoka*, and *haiga* journal *Prune Juice*.

www.prunejuice.wordpress.com

Postmodernism has failed. What was once an elite intellectual movement has become, in many instances, an insipid relativism in which there are no accepted standards. It may seem odd in a book on *senryu*, *kyoka*, and *haiga* to talk about standards, but a simple three-line poem in English that is solely humorous, for example, is not a *senryu*.

Combined with that, deconstructionism has also failed, or perhaps done its job too well — there is nothing left to deconstruct. It's time to rebuild. I hope this book can be part of a new literary movement. I hope communities with certain commonalities can come together and re-create literature and art together in a new and exciting way. It's time for originality and creativity once again. I hope the text now can mean something once again, rather than serve as an opportunity to deconstruct.

The poets in this book and I have no wish to enter the current scholarly debate about *senryu* and *kyoka*. Rather, we hope to learn from it. Our positions are tentative and perspectival.

We are open to criticism of the positive kind that increases the desire to learn more. We offer this book as an opportunity for all people to learn about *senryu*, *kyoka*, and *haiga* and to enjoy the process. I, at least, think that is a good thing.

# Treading Tentatively with *senryu*

by
Susan Campion

*Presenting one's self in a spontaneous, truthful, funny and/or profound way whilst also arousing a recognition of the reader's own human nature is the not-so-simple key to being a good writer of senryu.*

– Liam Wilkinson *Prune Juice* (November 2011)

Short, simple, to the point. Perhaps a one-liner. Seventeen syllables or less with satire or irony describing a human condition. Maybe 5-7-5? Maybe not. Think it's easy? Think it is yet defined as an English Language (EL) poetic form? No.

As Dr. Gabi Greve of the Daruma Museum, Japan, writes:

*senryu*
*don't tell me this is*
*a haiku*

And there lies the crux of the controversy. Are *senryu* and *haiku* two separate genres? We will leave that decision up to you.

Hiroaki Sato (2003) writes: "The distinction between the two genres (*senryu* and *haiku*) has been tenuous…from early on. In recent years, the blurring of the differences has become such that Onishi Yasuyo has said: "If someone asks me how *senryu* differ from *haiku*, I tell the inquirer that the only distinction that can be made is by author's name - that is, if the author is known to write *haiku*, the pieces he or she writes are *haiku*; if the author is known to write *senryu*, the pieces she or he writes are *senryu*."

Other respected writers offer varying opinions about a definition of *senryu* as a separate genre. William Pinckard, author of *Some senryu About Go,* suggests *senryu* "is a unique literary form that explores and expresses the nature of *avidya* (absence of brightness) and its manifestations in human life." Chen-ou Liu, respected *haiku* poet, suggests a definition based on the work of Makota Ueda: "the disuse of cutting combined with a thematic focus on human nature and folly conveyed through a satirical/humorous tone might constitute a workable definition of *senryu*."

Each writer in this book has wrestled long and hard to learn how to share 'pieces of her mind' about being women in three of several centuries-old short Japanese poetic forms, *senryu, kyoka* and *haiga*. These three forms were selected with reason and we have struggled to understand the forms well.

*Senryu* became an acknowledged short Japanese form, dating back to 1746, when men chose to use satire and irony to comment on their observations of human conditions. The precise definition of *senryu* suggests its colorful origins. The word itself means "river willow," which was slang for "prostitute." The origin of the form is largely attributed to Karai Senryu (1718-90), the pen name of Karai Hachiemon, who held contests to complete *senryu* poems. The form has largely been dominated by men throughout the ages and *senryu* clubs in Japan still exist.

Today, in the English Language (EL) *haiku* world, outspoken advocates of *haiku* would like to subsume the *senryu* form under the title of *haiku* - or, define *senryu* in ways that visually make the form/genre different from *haiku* (e.g., three lines, 5-7-5 syllable count, begin with a capital letter and end with a period, do not include a seasonal *kigo* or a cutting *kire,* perhaps maybe, even make the color different.)

We choose not to enter that debate.

The best we can do at this point in time is to quote Ray Rasmussen (raysweb.net): "A word of warning. If you are looking for a definitive answer to the question: What is *senryu* and how does it differ from *haiku*, you will not find it here."

Rather, we, as a group of women who have studied the forms, choose to remain out of the controversy and simply offer a description of *senryu*, rather than a definition, and offer you examples.

The women writers in this book have chosen to honor Japanese history, tradition, and aesthetics around *senryu*.

We are wise in that we continue to consider ourselves learners, and we are witty because we love to have fun with words in a satiric and ironic fashion.

We consider ourselves to be contemporary women who have analyzed and deconstructed history and dialogue both about feminism and Japanese short forms, but prefer to construct a new way of thinking - and, perhaps a new dialogue.

Our description of *senryu* and what guided us in our work is:

*Senryu is a short poetic form of Japanese origin with a smooth, not staccato, flow that focuses on humans or the human condition in an often ironic, cynical, sharply witty, or satiric manner.*

In this book, you will find *senryu* of two, three and four lines, and of various syllable counts per line. All of these poems will fit within the description above.

# Mad, Crazy and Wild Poems: *kyoka*

by

Carol Judkins

*Kyoka* are mad, crazy or wild poems, depending on the translation of the word.

These poems have a long history in Japanese literature, going in and out of favor sparked by political change and cultural sensibilities in Japan. Since we have included modern English Language *kyoka* written by our women authors in this compilation, we wish to present a little background.

*Kyoka* is often described as *tanka*'s stepsister. These poems are very different in tone to the refined elegance of traditional *waka*, now called *tanka*. During the early first centuries of the Heian period in Japan (794-1185), these mad poems were dismissed as throw-away *tanka* because they dealt with mundane matters and low culture. Imperial Court *tanka* was written in a manner faithful to the values of the Japanese aesthetic and high culture norms.

A few hundred years later, in the last centuries of the Edo Period (1100-1868), political and cultural changes in Japan created a context for *kyoka* poetry to flourish. These poems used colloquial language and often dealt with bawdy subject matter.

Samurai and commoners alike wrote these wild poems.

After 1868, *kyoka* poetry once again fell into disfavor due largely to political pressures.

Classical exemplars of *kyoka* are hard to find because so many of these poems were written and then thrown away. There are *kyoka* verse books preserved in museums and *ukiyo-e* woodblock prints with *kyoka* poems available to view.

'Licensed houses,' prostitutes, and kabuki theater actors were often the subjects of artwork and of *kyoka* poetry. Check our reading list if you are interested in exploring these classical exemplars.

Structurally, *kyoka* are *tanka*-like. English Language *kyoka* is usually written in five lines, employing 31 syllables or less, with a 5-7-5-7-7 syllable count or less. Just as in *tanka*, a pivot line or turn is often a feature, though not a requirement. The rules for *kyoka* are quite flexible. Most published English Language *kyoka* employ less than 31 syllables, which reflects an understanding that the Japanese 'on' sound unit is much shorter than with English syllables.

There are three styles of *kyoka* poetry. In the first, the poet follows all the traditional rules of *tanka* but creates a comical poem. In the second, an artistic feel is attempted while using slang and colloquial expressions. In the third, a familiar poem is parodied, which may require the reader to have a bit of background in history or classical literature. In all three styles, the use of allusion, the use of slang language, the employment of humor, satire, parody, irony, absurdity and word play is fair game.

Characterization of *kyoka* has been energetically discussed in English Language *tanka* print and on-line journals. The current thinking ranges from a view of it as an innovative expansion of the subject matter and tone, fit for modern English *tanka,* to *anti-tanka,* where it is seen as a separate genre that pokes holes in *tanka* pretensions, just as poets did in the Japanese early Heian and late Edo periods. There is a small but growing body of English Language *kyoka* poetry published today. Wise and witty women authors are perfect conduits to energize this mad poetry.

Here is a short poem I wrote to capture what I think is the essence of this modern style with a woman's sensibility:

> *silk fan*
> *dances in the dark*
> *kyoka*
> *a whiff of feminine scents*
> *in unconventional turns*

A silk fan is an iconic Japanese image. 'Dances in the dark' is a colloquial expression open to a variety of meanings. Literally, the fan twirls, but the phrase 'dances in the dark' does have a bawdy connotation, too. Lady Gaga and Bruce Springsteen say it well. As we share their thoughts in this mad, crazy, wild form of poetry, we hope you enjoy the unique perspectives women bring to the dance.

# *haiga*

by
Suzanne Fuller

The Japanese *haiga* is a simple yet profound observation of the everyday world. Usually humorous or ironic, it often contains a juxtaposition of a *haiku* or a *senryu* and an image. The image can also complement the verse by reinforcing its imagery. Traditional Japanese *haiga* drawings were restrained with minimal ink, minimal color and very light brush work. They often had a light feel with a touch of irony or amusement even if the subject of the verse was serious.

*While the haiku and the painting in a haiga share the same space, they are meant to complement, and not explain, one another. In fact, in some cases the haiku and the painting have nothing to do with one another, because, explains Takiguchi,* (SusumuTakiguchi, founder of *World Haiku Club*): *"if the painting and haiku are similar, it would mean that one has been added because the other is not adequate." This would not only be redundant, he says, but could even be perceived as rude...The third element of haiga-calligraphy determines the look of the poem on the page and communicates its essence.*[1.]

Japanese calligraphy is a stunning art form in itself and in the traditional *haiga,* it is an integral element of the overall design. The characters are grouped in a block that is designed and placed as a separate, elegant design element in graceful balance with the illustration.

In contemporary *haiga*, line illustrations are still used, as well as photography and graphic designs. Unless the poet is Japanese, most writers do not use Japanese calligraphy, but **do** use typography that can, in the same way, add something extra to the design and enhance meaning. The calligraphy—the verse—in a traditional *haiga* was typically drawn in a block in one place. Many contemporary *haiga* display the type in a more playful manner as you will see in some of the examples of *senryu haiga* in this collection. I love the *haiga* form—visual sound bites of sardonic wisdom!

I am a graphic designer and illustrator by profession, so solving visual communications puzzles is great fun for me and creating an illustration for a *haiga* is very much like editorial illustration. In this *haiga* example *I try to ignore*, I wanted to point up the humor of the verse with an image that juxtaposed it. I tried out several image ideas that could illustrate **not** ignoring the old man. The binoculars seemed perfect.

*I try to ignore*

*the old man*

*in the Speedo*

—*contributed by Suzanne Fuller*

[1.] www.poets.org: *The Haiga: Haiku, Calligraphy and Painting*

# 美Beauty
## on face value

美
悟
笑
情
力
真
知
友

*falling stars—*
*whose are these*
*saggy breasts?*
　　—Furrow


*middle-aged*
*skin's elasticity*
*has abandoned ship*
　　—Bickel


*the melting moments*
*of chocolate gorging*
*won't melt thunder thighs*
　　—Kammer

*wearing Dad's jeans*
*reminds me of how*
*his genes wear me*
—Corum


*when losing twenty pounds,*
*my hind end isn't the problem*
*my middle's the ass*
—Bonnell


*lite salad dressing*
*has only 10 calories*
*cheesecake for dessert*
—Fuller

*swimsuit time*
*is a harrowing experience*
*she suns in the bathtub*
—Bickel

*my beach body*
*seeks*
*winter cover-up*
—Kammer

*thirty-day diet*
*is the answer to my prayers*
*ten days lost so far*
—Stockwell

girls at the mall
buy red stilettos
a legal high
—Furrow


feeling expansive,
I sign up
for zumba class
—Judkins


for my life to change
first I must change—
what will I wear?
—Kammer

*twilight turns vampires*
*into horror-movie heartthrobs*
*sexy shape-shifters*
—Stern

*school uniform*
*versus skin tight yoga pants*
*bum debate*
—Noel

naked
as a flower
without her petals

**Marie Toole**

*bread dough*
*rising on the stove—*
*I gasp*
*it looks so much*
*like my belly*
—Judkins

*was trying*
*to get*
*into shape*
*couldn't choose*
*which one*
—Toole

*real ladies*
*never laugh*
*at dirty jokes*
*at least*
*not in public*
—Chiechi

*a pencil skirt*
*husband eyes*
*its knee length*
*and asks*
*"What's the point?"*
—Furrow


*she dons*
*her low-cut, tight*
*black satin negligee*
*then turns out*
*the light*
—Judkins


*Men-a-pause*
*they're confused*
*why does lack of sex drive*
*make women*
*hot and sweaty?*
—Ross

*windswept willow trees*
*breaking their backs*
*reminds me*
*of my hour*
*in the gym*
—Toole

*less sparkle*
*in my eyes these days—*
*a sure sign*
*the webcam*
*needs adjusting*
—Judkins

*mirror mirror*
*clever master of disguise*
*beauty magician*
*who conceals lines and wrinkles*
*by just closing your eyes*
—Stockwell

## Just One Voice
by
Suzanne Fuller

How did I come to have a voice in this collection? Like everything in life, it was a journey down a path directed not by me, but by one small decision after another, a little turn in this direction and then a pull in that. I have always enjoyed writing, always enjoyed *words*, but have only recently begun writing poetry. I have always been an avid reader of many genres: fiction, biography, science, history and essay, but never of poetry. I found so much of it obscure and difficult to understand. One day my husband gave me a collection of poems by Mary Oliver and I was enchanted. I was inspired to learn to read and enjoy poetry and thought the best way to do that would be to sign up for a poetry writing class.

I took several classes that explored the different elements of poetry. Participating in the writing exercises completely opened up this world for me. I began to read poetry of all sorts and appreciate and understand it. But this was just one of those little turns. I discovered that I really wanted to learn to *write* good poetry and to explore all genres.

My next exploration led me to classes in Japanese short forms—*haiku, senryu, kyoka, tanka* and *haiga*. I hoped that this exercise would teach me the craft of expressing an idea or an image with minimal words; I admire the technique of choosing those essential words, no more, no less, that would move a reader with beautiful and profound simplicity. These classes met every expectation. Any skill I learned by practicing these Japanese forms will carry over into all of my writing and improve it.

I think of myself as just a writer. I don't think of myself as a *woman* writer. But I think it is my woman's sensitivity to the astounding mysteries and stunning beauty of the natural world that informs so much of my writing. So, of course, I found the Japanese forms, especially the *haiku* which is traditionally steeped in seasonal images, very appealing.

However, when it came to *senryu,* I felt really challenged. I do not think myself at all funny but I discovered the form is perfectly suited to my cynical and sarcastic sense of humor, my desire to point up the ridiculous. Perhaps because I am most comfortable in the natural world, and I look out at the world from there, I see the flaws and foibles of humankind from a removed perspective. Writing *senryu* lets me express my dismay at our misguided concepts and behaviors in a fun way; seen from the eyes of other creatures we must be a hilarious bunch. It gives me a stage for my voice of protest, and if I do it well, perhaps I can influence someone else's small turn.

## My Life is an Open Book

by
Marie Toole

I have been writing for as long as I can remember, scribbling notes in class, hiding my poems in my schoolbooks and keeping journals of writings that later became poetry. Not all are as cute and comical as what I have learned in our senryu classes.

My whole life is written down in some fashion, either as a short story, essay, or in a poem. Some would say that my life is an open book.

Luckily for me, I have a sense of humor that flows into my writing and creates an interest for an audience. I consider myself fortunate to have a unique personality. Maybe being from Brooklyn has something to do with it or maybe it's just a gift from God.

Writing has always been a passion of mine, and now that I am retired, I have more time to devote to it. My special love is *senryu*, in which you can take an ordinary, everyday occurrence and turn it into a funny outlook on life. Every day is a new beginning for me because I never know what will come out next.

I loved journalism class and worked on the school newspaper staff in high school. In recent years, I've written for magazines, local newspapers, and even have my own Poetry Corner in *Center For Writing Excellence*, an online newsletter.

Some *senryu* and *kyoka* were accepted by *Prune Juice* and some essays I wrote were printed in *Vocalpoint*.

When I worked for our local "Good News" newspaper, *The Happy Herald*, I was the celebrity interviewer and met with Dixie Carter, Eric Estrada, Ed McMahon, George Hamilton, Carol Channing, and many more distinguished stars. The editor of the *Herald* also asked me to write my own cooking column, which later prompted me to write a cookbook called *Keeping the Tradition*. My recipes have been featured in the *Palm Beach Post*, the *Saturday Evening Post* and in *Cooking Club of America*.

# 悟Enlightenment
## "Aha!" says she

美悟笑情力真知友

*showering*
*with my glasses on*
*morning fog*
—Bonnell


*the dog*
*wolfs his supper, belches—*
*I don't miss you*
—Fuller


*a rainy day*
*provokes moody thoughts*
*and scattered showers*
—Corum

*singing birds*
*assemble on a wire*
*choir practice*
—Creager

*ICU lounge –*
*two cell phone chargers*
*in every outlet*
—Funk

*not heard of I.D.—*
*Inattention Disorder*
*married males' disease*
—Stern

*rippled lake*
*image of an older me*
*looks back*
—Furrow


*alone*
*in a room full*
*of people*
—Bonnell


*human arrogance*
*Earth's court gives verdict*
*on judgment errors*
—Marshall

*the people*
*dining out*
*went in*
        —Bonnell


*granddaughter teaches*
*what I'd forgotten*
*about playing jacks*
        —Funk


*on a wacky whim,*
*I step into a playground*
*find myself at eight*
        —Creager

*caterpillar claims*
*cocoon's a comfy home*
*butterfly says jail*
—Marshall

*good ending—*
*too bad it didn't start*
*sooner in the play*
—Stern

*aria*
*in the bathtub*
*suds fall flat*
—Furrow

dinner guests —
we discuss the famine
in Somalia

**Carol Judkins**

*my dinner plate*
*so congested*
*I need a road map*
*to find*
*the roast*
—Creager

*as siblings squabble*
*over Mom's heirloom pearls*
*I reach for her box*
*with food-stained recipes*
*that define her legacy*
—Chiechi

*deeply satisfied women*
*agree at length*
*not all fake plastic*
*is uncomfortable*
*widely accepted*
—Ross

*his nightmare—*
*he cannot*
*get it up*
*with a*
*willing female*
—Bickel


*for years I was known*
*as Johnny and Jenny's mom*
*till the nest emptied*
*I cried, then rejoiced*
*I had a name again*
—Chiechi

## I'm A Wanderer

by
Nancy Bravo Creager

I'm a wanderer. I like to wander into unknowns. I was a premature baby and couldn't wait to wander into this world. I like to see and feel what is up there, beyond my eyes—beyond my skies. This has always been my passion, to go, to feel, to experience life at its fullest.

As a woman, and as a mother, I didn't have the luxury of wandering into many places, so books became my magic carpet. They were my quiet and faithful friends. Besides, I like privacy and the companionship of books. Enlacing my fingers in their covers and leafing around pages brought a feeling of blazing anticipation. Yes, I read much. It gives me a sense of joy and exhilaration, the thrill of trespassing through times, space, cultures. I don't need to leave home to live the impossible.

I started reading to escape a lonely and closed-in childhood. In the cold of my Spartan room I could hold a book and it would transport me to a warm and florid sunset. Reading invited me to write—asking me to give my take on what I was reading, to breathe out what I was inhaling. It made me feel important, that I mattered. It gave me a wonderful feeling of completeness, especially when hardly anybody paid attention to me.

My awakening day came in third grade. Our teacher announced a contest: to write about something we liked, or something that was important to us. Out of my memory materialized a shady fig tree that grew in my grandmother's yard, the ripe figs falling on the ground, and the sweet and grainy feel in my mouth, the remembrance of a very simple joy. No, I didn't win the contest. But I received an Honorable Mention and for a moment I felt lifted up from the ground, sort of floating between the blackboard and the teacher. I wonder if that is the feeling an honored writer receives when accepting the Nobel Prize.

In my teenage years I discovered poetry. Pablo Neruda was the first to inspire me. Under his light, I wrote my first love poem to a boy who played basketball in the street where I lived. At the mere sight of him, emotions surged within me like a flood—quite shocking. By the way, he never knew I existed.

After high school, I had the opportunity to travel abroad and I took the challenge, though barely knowing English. I was quite ready to wander in real life by then, and in a breath I crossed mountains and seas. I wallowed in the new culture like a kid in a candy store. I got married.

I raised four children in quick succession, and for a while I was happy raising a family of my own. I belonged to someone now, and I stopped wandering. I was doing my best to let my children know they were wanted and loved. My reading became children's stories, and my writing, my grocery list.

After a couple of years, I started wandering again. Close by was a school that offered night classes. I enrolled, delighted and scared at the same time. I took basic courses in English grammar and composition, and later on, I challenged myself to learn basic accounting to get a paying job to help support the family. I felt young and ready to wander into different subjects. In time, I worked as an accounting clerk and later as an administrative assistant.

As years went by I came back to reading and writing. I have much to catch up on. One of my wishes is to write a book for my family—sort of vignettes of my life—a mix of poetry and prose. I am collecting those raindrops.

I concentrate mostly on poetry these days, wandering through different styles and genres. It keeps my mind challenged and my spirit alive.

Now I've embraced the Japanese style of poetry. I admire the concentration of its thoughts and the definitiveness of its words.

## Retirement to Poetry

by

Joan E. Stern

Following the tradition of many women, I was an accommodator regarding my family. I took my parenting responsibilities very seriously, and waited until my child was three before going back to work part-time. From then on, I used to say I painted every ten years, since there was rarely spare time.

Fast forward three decades to four years ago, when I saw the graffiti on the economic wall. I spent many soul-searching hours contemplating retirement from my job as a business consultant, since I feared I would lose my identity if I stopped working. Ultimately, I chose to leave on a high note, since consulting, like security and advertising, although quite important, tended to be the first costs to be stripped when budgets got tight. The last thing I wanted was to find myself downsized by a failed economy.

The day after the big "R," my secret weapon was to start six classes designed for seniors at Emeritus College. It was summer session, which was only six weeks in length, and one of the offerings was creative writing. Exploring something so different sounded like fun, and I knew that even if I hated the course, I could endure almost anything for such a short time period.

The instructor allowed us to write assignments in prose or poetry. For some unknown reason, I wrote the first one as a rhymed poem. Her response was, "If you are serious about this gig, you need to write every day." That first poem was published by our local newspaper, causing me to take this idea of writing for myself more seriously and motivating me to accommodate myself by honing my craft.

I continue to attempt to develop my signature, and I enjoy *senryu* because of its intense distillation of ideas and feelings in either a serious or light-hearted vein.

I still find it extraordinary to have discovered a new passion at age sixty-five. Now, I have reduced the course load to four, paint once a week, and write poetry every day.

# 笑Laughter
## naughty but nice

美悟笑情力真知友

*hungry Mary*
*stopped at a restaurant*
*she had a little lamb*
—Yocom


*casino skywalk*
*old lady with cane*
*outsprints us*
—Funk


*in the dark I grab*
*my warm fuzzy blanket*
*the dog growls*
—Bonnell

*two prudes in bed*
*undress*
*chewing gum*
—Creager


*he circles*
*for the space*
*near the gym door*
—Fuller


*the exorcist won*
*but the man refused to pay*
*he's been repossessed*
—Yocom

*lost, he doubles back*
*without asking directions*
*man behind the wheel*
—Funk

*maybe*
*in a way, I'm sort of*
*indecisive*
—Fuller

*in a prickly mood,*
*my son asks the balloon man*
*for a porcupine*
—Judkins

*dollar store brags*
*everything you need's a buck -*
*where's the gas pump?*
—Stockwell


*main street cordoned off*
*one carload of clowns*
*heads the wrong way*
—Funk


*the sharp baker*
*shows off his new invention—*
*a four-loaf cleaver*
—Yocom

*murdered*
*in my kitchen*
*a beet*
—Bonnell


*the forger escaped*
*from state prison*
*a slip of the pen*
—Yocom


*everyone laughs*
*at Father's bawdy jokes*
*Mother just rolls her eyes*
—Noel

*Dead End*
*says the sign*
*at the dead end*
—Fuller


*life*
*is too short*
*sprint*
—Stern


*tintype portrait*
*someone's ancestor*
*with a price*
*on his head*
—Funk

*Santa said*
*"Ho, ho, ho."*
*I slapped him silly*
—Toole


*kleptomania*
*when it gets out of control*
*I just take something*
—Stockwell


*I'm reading a book*
*all about levitation*
*I can't put it down*
—Yocom

*In a yoga pose*

*I breathe peace*

*but lose dignity*

**Robyn  Corum**

*making love*
*under our down comforter*
*a feather floats by*
*and a sneeze*
*comes*
—Bonnell


*he talks with his hands*
*it isn't sign language*
*but a habit*
*he picked up*
*in Italy*
—Toole


*bitter morning*
*fresh snow decorates*
*yesterday's ice*
*in my hurry I become*
*an accidental angel*
—Fuller

*kids hatch*
*breakfast plot*
*lace Mum's bran*
*with corn relish*
*cereal killers*
—Ross

*my perfect dresser*
*with four tall roomy drawers*
*skirts and blouses revered*
*last shelf*
*unmatched socks*
—Creager

*when I finally*
*had a handle*
*on my life*
*it broke*
*off the door*
—Toole

## Farts, Vomit and Bugs

by
Melissa Bickel

Humor, to me, is a cross between deadpan and jovial. I tend to believe humor is used mostly by women. Life is demanding, and a woman has many different roles she plays on any given day, so humor is a must to survive.

I've been a single mom since my son was twelve. I had to learn to be the mother and father in certain circumstances. In this sort of role, humor is needed. One example is puberty.

When my son entered puberty, if my sense of humor hadn't been intact, I'd have gone insane. Some of the things I learned about a young boy's rite of passage, physically and emotionally, were gross.

I am now familiar with terminology equated to a young boy's body parts. Herman and German are not references to names or nationalities. These terms are used when referring to what hangs down south.

Also, anything to do with farts, vomit and bugs is funny and cool when you're a young boy — even now to grown men it seems. My now twenty-year old still finds humor in the creepy and disgusting.

God knew what he was doing when he created women to bring life into the world and nurture babies and children. If a man breast-fed, he'd go around squirting his friends with milk.

For me, humor is a part of my poetry, my prose and certainly a part of my life. My humor is textured and layered on so many different planes of life experiences. It's what has kept me sane. Humor has allowed me to laugh in the face of adversity and has let me become far stronger, emotionally, than I thought I'd ever be.

*he made me laugh*
*blowing milk through his nose*
*I kissed his face*

# The Life I Love

by
Karyn Stockwell

Writing is like breathing to me. It's a vital part of who I am, and I can't imagine a single day without digging into my imagination and my soul to capture those ideas in the form of prose or poetry. It's a passion I never want to surrender.

Yet, when asked to write an essay about being a woman writer, I couldn't help but wonder if anyone would want to read about my life. Nevertheless, I shall write.

Writing gives me a vast opportunity to convey, in any format I desire, what I feel in any given moment about any given topic. I've dabbled in non-fiction and explored mystery and crime stories, sports-related tales, horror and thriller prose. In addition, I've explored a variety of poetry formats, romance, and mature pieces. I find myself embracing and frequently exploring my sense of humor.

I seek out opportunities to laugh every day and strive to make others laugh with me. So often, when we are consumed by activities of life, we overlook the funny things people do or say and thus fail to perceive all the humorous possibilities in our lives.

*"A keen sense of humor helps us overlook the unbecoming, understand the unconventional, tolerate the unpleasant, overcome the unexpected, and outlast the unbearable."*

-Billy Graham

Knowing something I've written has tickled someone enough to smile or laugh brings an incomparable feeling. When I discovered the irony and satire of *senryu*, I thought I'd died and gone to heaven. There is no better praise for me, as a *senryu* writer, than having a reader tell me my poem made them smile, giggle, chuckle, or laugh.

To me, life is a *senryu*. The form embraces nature, people, humor, emotions, and enlightenment. It relays a moment when I hold my breath, grab my enthusiasm by its socks, and know without a doubt that I can find so much in life to celebrate. I hope I will forever maintain a child's sense of wonder and humor, for children have no boundaries and respond to the events of life with true emotion.

Often, writing flows like some unseen keyboardist has taken over my fingers. I've come to love and depend on the poet in my soul, who says with brevity what a million prose words couldn't possibly convey. Although I love writing both poetry and prose, I really want to keep learning about humor in my writing. As a result, I'll continue to learn more about myself, and the life I enjoy.

*"Humor is mankind's greatest blessing."*

-Mark Twain

## Humor

by

Sally Yocom

Humor should be an important part of everyone's life. It is all around us, if we just look for it. I find it sometimes in unexpected places.

"Instructions: Remove baby from stroller before folding." My electric iron has a setting for permanent press. The sign at a nearby bank's parking lot says: "Illegal parking not permitted." Another sign on campus says: "No am or pm parking. Parking with permit allowed at other times." A notice from a magazine begins: "Dear recently expired subscriber..." A newspaper classified ad says: "4-year-old babysitter needed." Another ad says: "For sale. Pet Goat. Will eat anything. Loves children." A signboard says: "Crash courses for training pilots."

Much humor is deliberate. A diaper service truck announces: "Rock a Dry Baby." A sign on a southern street says: "No U-all turn."

Humor is a gift. Be on the lookout for it. Anything that brings a smile or laugh raises the spirits and is conducive to good health. Tell the world: "Humor me."

Humor is not only a major form of entertainment— its power has been proven to be a secret weapon for healing both our bodies and our minds. "Laughter is the best medicine" is not an old wives' tale—it's a fact. Laughter decreases pain, builds the immune system, and lowers stress.

Humor can change our outlook and make life's troubles seem a wee bit smaller. Laughter helps us overcome our fears, except for snakes - there's nothing funny about snakes.

Laughter helps us take our lives and ourselves less seriously. We all need the wonderful side effects of humor. It sparks our imagination. I know I can use some more sparks in my life.

You can't be sad while you're laughing. Try it. It's impossible.

A sense of humor gives us a chance to turn negativity into healing, positive attitudes. We can laugh at ourselves, get others to laugh with us, and maybe get them to laugh at themselves, too.

Laughter is contagious. Sometimes, even if we don't think something is funny, we'll laugh in response to the sound of another person's laughter.

As a woman, I feel I have a different sense of humor than men. It's neither a good thing nor a bad thing, just different. Many would say it's because we have to deal with men and teenagers, but I think it's to help us maintain some sanity in a world of continuous craziness.

# 情 Passion

## I have a headache

美悟笑情力真知友

A *senryu* Suite

*butter melts*
*on corn on the cob*
*I lick it*

*barbecued*
*New York steaks now stew*
*thanks to you*

*you ask for*
*favorite ice cream cake*
*cherry's on the top*

*under sheets*
*whipped cream swirls -*
*go to sleep*
—Campion

*I bake bread*
*to see something rise*
*in the morning*
—Toole



*three-minute sex*
*we both dive*
*for the remote*
—Kammer



*hot flashes*
*she douses the flames*
*with frozen daiquiris*
—Fuller

*when morning cradles you,*
*your reposing body wakes*
*I fade away*
—Bickel


*empty arms*
*leave unfulfilled promises*
*bitter womb*
—Corum


*snowman*
*grins with lusty delight—*
*snowblower's coming.*
—Stockwell

*silver-haired ladies*
*spot new man at senior home*
*sixteen again*
—Chiechi

*odometer starts*
*to turn up zeroes*
*his gentle nudge*
—Funk

*his pillow*
*the memory of him*
*suffocates me*
—Furrow

*he moved in*
*with baggage*
*no suitcases*
—Toole

*I wish my man*
*held me - instead, he caresses*
*remote*
—Kammer

*Viagra thief*
*deserves stiff penalty*
*hardened criminal*
—Noel

*I have long forgotten*
*my locker number*
*the color of your eyes*
—Corum


*on blind date*
*I beg the waiter*
*"Please, kill me..."*
—Stockwell


*barren fruit tree—*
*your hand slips off*
*my belly*
—Furrow

her buttons pushed
he was shown the couch
        with no blankets

**Melissa Bickel**

*gear shift*
*on the floor*
*old husband*
*back to young tricks*
*playing with my knee*
—Funk

*still trying to open*
*these damned plastic bags*
*visions of the produce guy*
*his eyes bulge, his head sweats*
*but he fits*
—Bickel

*he can read my thoughts*
*I complete his sentences*
*now we look alike*
*thirty-five years of marriage*
*and not too old to be cloned*
—Chiechi

*kyoka* Suite

*your toes*
*brush my bare feet*
*rhythmically;*
*small jolts build in places*
*long lost to memories*

*your fingers*
*dance on my skin*
*playfully;*
*images emerge*
*of you entering me*

*reality*
*still suffices as pleasure*
*realistically;*
*you offer your love to me*
*in the only way you can now*

*blossoms open*
*to accept a honeybee*
*hungrily*
*who wants to give back to the plant*
*a gift for the nectar it soon receives*
—Campion

*we make hot love*
*in the semi-privacy*
*of our bedroom*
*with just one spectator,*
*our dog who yawns a lot*
—Chiechi


*John Deere tractor man*
*with all the right parts*
*rolls and swaggers the field*
*my grass is wet*
*oh dear, John Deere man*
—Creager


*I wish my man*
*made love*
*with the passion*
*he gives*
*the remote*
—Kammer

*few good men*
*find a woman's treasure*
*x does not*
*mark the spot*
*throwaway map*
—Ross


*snuggled in bed*
*I feel his gentle touch*
*tingles erupt*
*anticipation builds*
*before I hear his soft snores*
—Campion


*we were in the throes*
*of a passionate embrace*
*his heart was in the right place*
*how I wished his hands and mouth*
*would do the same*
—Toole

## An Erma Bombeck Passion

by
Connie Chiechi

I like to think I'm funny. No one enjoys my sense of humor more than I do; at least, that's what my husband often tells me. Does he not get my humor? My girlfriends do.

My women friends and I can chat and laugh for hours over things that often our men just don't seem to find amusing, or perhaps they don't relate. For example, one evening among couples, we women came up with ingenious ways to describe to our husbands what it's like to have one of those dreaded mammograms. One woman compared it to a tire driving over a penis, and all the women laughed. The men did not. Why not try to make light of something that just might be painful. Perhaps, at times, humor is our way of coping.

For as long as I can remember, I have wanted to write, but life always seemed to get in the way - not in a bad way, though. Between going to graduate school, working full time, and raising a family, there just didn't seem to be any "me" time left at the end of the day to write. And if I did happen to have a spare few minutes late at night, I was too tired to think.

For years, I kept a journal off and on and took a few creative writing courses, both in college and through a correspondence class, always savoring those moments when I could be creative. And somewhere along the way, as I was assuming all the roles in my life, I discovered the musings and delightful humor of the late Erma Bombeck in her book, *Family-The Ties that Bind and Gag.* She looked at life from the perspective of a mother and wife by providing humorous and sometimes what I considered to be satirical views of family life in the eighties.

After reading a few of her books, I knew I wanted to write just like Ms. Bombeck. All these years, she has been one of my greatest inspirations. While I've not yet achieved her status and will most likely never do so, the most memorable compliment one member of my on-line writing group once told me was that some of my writing reminded her of Erma Bombeck. She had no idea how much I revered Bombeck's writing style and wit.

Once retired, I finally found time to write. Interestingly, though, while I set out to write short stories and essays, my focus quickly turned to poetry, and poetry is now my passion.

## Passion's Journey

by
Deborah C. Kammer

A metaphor for my life six months ago might well have been a "Mack-truck moment."

I have heard that life gives one taps on the shoulder— if not heeded, then in comes the Mack truck, all eighteen wheels. I guess I might be considered a slow learner in some areas. I needed the full, head-on, wheel crunching, crashing moment.

As a result of life crashing in, I sought the peace of a reclusive life to meditate and contemplate where to find the right path, preferably free of heavy traffic. I had always been a prolific writer, relating to reports or technical subjects. By accident, I joined a writer's site.

The creative aspects of writing appealed to me. I wanted to write poetry. I had always loved reading it, yet had not considered myself to have any ability. Questioning what to write and how to get started, I wrote my first *haiku* in the 5-7-5 syllable count as I was incorrectly advised a *haiku* should be written.

*write a masterpiece*
*not easy to find the words*
*pen to paper start*

Wow, I could write a poem. Maybe not the best poem, and definitely not a *haiku*, but I had to start somewhere. What appealed to me was that so much could be said in so few words. I did feel the constrictive pressure of the defined syllable count. What appealed was the gentle breath of this age-old Japanese form that I read first in Japanese works and then in more modern work, which adhered to the Japanese aesthetic. The unfinished element took my breath away.

I saw it in the talented work of others. I saw it in the famous published writers of these forms and felt myself drawn to the Japanese aesthetic and the ancient philosophy and wisdom contained in these difficult and clever writing forms.

Writing short poetry is not as easy as it sounds. There are many rules to this type of poetry. I wanted more than anything to know how to get it right.

After reading work by Alvin Thomas Ethington, I took his class on the Shorter Poetic Forms. *Haiku* first, then *senryu*. I was enraptured. What a way to express my feelings and how I see the world in satire, irony, playfulness and hysterical wit.

I have discovered the hard way that the status quo needs questioning and there is much suffering and injustice inflicted by peer pressure to conform. This is where I see change is needed and this is where my writing passion is leading.

Reflecting on the human condition has become more perilous. Most writers comment on the human condition, or raise issues to ponder, with their own interpretations. I believe this is the importance of this book.

We women want to be up-front about what is happening to our society and to convey thoughts on how we see the world. We may not all agree on certain themes, yet we have in common a sense of fun, humor, and love of the shorter forms of Japanese poetry.

The forms in this book had been traditionally associated with men. These poems are not necessarily the polite and conservative comments women have, in the past, been expected to make.

They all contain satire or irony and are told in ways perhaps sometimes bawdy, definitely witty and thigh slapping in many instances. Though not always funny, they can be 'knowing,' contain wisdom, and offer commentary. All are based on the human condition. At the very least, they can be termed playful. At their utmost, they can be hair-raising.

# 力Strength

nego-she-ator

美 悟 笑 情 力 真 知 友

*veterans' clinic*
*wheelchair-bound comrades relive*
*old war movies*
—Funk


*tornado in cemetery*
*hundreds dead*
—Corum


*in fields*
*of abandoned homes*
*tent cities bloom*
—Bickel

*mammography—*
*tightening the grip*
*on breast cancer*
—Furrow

*first day of pre-school*
*I tie his shoestrings*
*ever so slowly*
—Chiechi

*why mess up one thing*
*when I can do more damage*
*multi-tasking*
—Toole

*cross-legged lady stands*
*outside locked restroom door*
*in a prayerful mood*
—Noel

*morning mosaic*
*hand-stitched quilt*
*and rumpled thoughts*
—Corum

*assertive women*
*found attractive*
*until they show their balls*
—Ross

*the dentist's drill*
*my grandmother's funeral*
—Corum

*mothers coax*
*magnificent music*
*from broken instruments*
—Marshall

*cyberchondriacs*
*constantly focused on health*
*on-line compulsion*
—Stern

*behind a diaper*
*Abuelita hides*
*a tear*
—Creager

*carried through the crowd*
*naked mannequin*
*stares straight ahead*
—Funk

*young mother rocks*
*in untouched nursery*
*broken willow limbs*
—Furrow

*dead body*
*litters doorway*
*bloody doormat*
—Kammer

*deep pain ripens*
*seeds of innate awareness*
*buds burst to blossom*
—Marshall

*vultures*
*pick the carcass*
*estate sale*
—Bonnell

*seniors' saggy boobs*
*create warm winter vests*
*old age benefits*
—Noel


*special day*
*even without candles*
*illuminates*
—Stern


*the actors toiled hard*
*but the show closed in one day*
*all work and no play*
—Yocom

the change
now he wears a jacket
in the house

**Suzanne Fuller**

scraped knee
of fallen toddler
requires
a Band-Aid
major surgery
—Ross


moms' night out -
caged birds
set free
till they fly home
to nurture
—Chiechi


solitary star
winks a midnight greeting
welcome love
I reach out to embrace
my memory foam pillow
—Stockwell

*winter night*
*a coyote yelps*
*and feeds its pups*
*I wake*
*to an empty chicken coop*
—Furrow

*lone monk*
*is quite proud*
*of his robe*
*without guidance,*
*he would never remove it*
—Marshall

*Mum's milk train*
*on time*
*pump connection*
*at twelve sharp*
*midnight express*
—Ross

*he walks away*
*without a glance*
*carries her heart*
*she cries in darkness*
*and smiles in the light*
—Corum

*mothers contain*
*an internal GPS*
*homing device with*
*pinpoint accuracy*
*"Mom. Where's my shoes ..."*
—Stockwell

*early morning*
*on first day*
*school bus headlights*
*spark this mother's tears*
—Funk

# Running Hurdles
## by
## Lois J. Funk

Six years of attending my son's track meets made me thankful that he'd chosen to keep his feet on the ground for sprints and relays, rather than running hurdles. Watching his fellow teammates tackle barrier after barrier kept a prayer on my lips that, win or lose, they would not stumble and if they did, that they could still finish the race.

At the same time I was praying for those young runners, I was running hurdles of my own in the writing field. My urge to write had been fueled years before by the encouragement of two English teachers.

My goal throughout high school had been to become a journalist. But my father's sudden and unexpected death, six months before graduation, destroyed my incentive for any further education. As a result, I came to my first hurdle—the underlying thought that without a degree of some kind I could never write anything worthwhile. Furthermore, even if I did, it might be recognized by my own little world of family and friends, but never by the reading world beyond them.

When family and friends encouraged me to seek a publisher for my work, I gingerly climbed over that first hurdle and stumbled on, along the track leading to the next one. It came in the form of a possible, but not probable, challenge. One *writer in the know* stated that stay-at-home housewives and moms, both titles I wear proudly, could possibly, but not probably, become successful writers. Sheer determination helped me knock down and trample that barrier with both feet. I would keep writing what I was capable of writing and tackle success later.

Then came the blunt realization that most editors/publishers weren't looking for, or even reading, poetry—especially traditional rhymed and metered verse, which was my passion, and which had already flowed into my children's stories. The only glimpse of hope came in yet another writer's suggestion: "If you can do it well, try it."

I did, and it worked, to a degree. My traditional poetry was now getting published and winning awards, but my stories were still sitting on the sidelines, where they stayed until I arrived at my next hurdle.

This time I read that for various reasons, children's stories could be harder to write and get published than any other writing. By now I knew both facts were absolutely true. But I was on a roll, and since I had gotten around the other hurdles, I could surely get around this one. I just needed to find an editor who was willing to read my children's stories *and* consider them for publication. That hurdle was cleared successfully when, over the next few years, the editor of a children's magazine purchased and published over eighty rhyming stories and poems written specifically for their needs. At the same time, another editor began accepting, and is still publishing, my inspirational children's stories.

Several years ago, a handwriting analyst pegged me as being determined in what I wish to accomplish. Had I balked at any one of the hurdles along my writing track, I might still be wishing I could write something worthy of publication. As it is, I can peer through the glass doors of my personal library and say, "Hey. Each of those publications holds one or more of my writings."

Of course, where there is a desire to learn, and another goal waiting on the sidelines; there will always be another hurdle to clear.

## A Busy Life

by

Nessie Noel

I feel I've led a life packed full of an amazing variety of interesting experiences and adventures.

After finishing high school, I trained as a laboratory technologist and worked for a few years in local hospitals.

Then, a friend and I saved our pennies and took a six-month tour of Europe. We stayed in hostels and roughed it, while driving through seventeen countries. Our tiny, rented, red Citroen was subject to breaking down in unusual places. We visited historical and cultural sites during this journey of discovery, all of which left strong and lasting impressions.

After arriving back in Canada, I spent three and a half years doing Christian Missionary work in various locations before meeting and marrying my husband. Over a period of eight years, we became the proud parents of six beautiful children. I remain ever-thankful for my kind, supportive husband and still miss him. He was far too young when he passed away.

In my 'spare' time, I raised and showed purebred Soft-Coated Wheaten Terriers and Cavalier King Charles Spaniels. Helping the bitches whelp their puppies was a particular joy and raising these adorable babies was fun and rewarding. I always found loving forever homes for the little guys and it was a special treat to hear back from their proud new owners.

One of my most enjoyable hobbies is making porcelain dolls. I enjoy every step of this process: pouring clay into molds, firing the clay, cracking the molds, painting the doll parts, re-firing them, and at last, assembling the dolls and sewing authentic period costumes for them. I learned to sculpt my own original dolls and to cast original molds for them, using the lost wax method learned from a world famous sculptor, Ron Booker, who was employed by Louis Tussaud's Wax Works in Niagara Falls, Ontario.

As a result of becoming a doll artisan under his tutorage, I was commissioned to sculpt, design, cast an original mold, and construct the prototype of a mass production porcelain doll.

More examples of my busy life: I love to paint and draw and enjoy working in acrylics and in pen and ink. My paintings and drawings depict homey scenes featuring families and country life.

Over the years, I've written dozens of poems. Most of these poems were never shared with others, though a few have been published in poetry anthologies. Finding online poetry sites has been a highlight in my life because it provides an opportunity to learn to write poetry in many styles and brings me into contact with several brilliant poets and poetesses whose constructive criticism helped improve my writing.

After living a very busy life, and now in my golden years, I'm currently allowing myself lots of time to be still, to observe, and to simply be.

# Talking the Talk

## by
## Phillippa Ross

I was born to talk. Yes, folks, I'm convinced I exited the womb talking. Seriously, people tell me I could talk under water with a mouth full of marbles, and with a small amount of training, I think I could prove it. As I explore my evolution, the inevitable polishing words would rub off as a career choice. I'd rack up a word count of ten thousand a day by the age of five. Coupled with that, two older brothers gave me a constant pounding, which would mean the development of a razor quick wit. So there I was, a little tadpole in a pond of words, and without knowing it, set on my path to becoming a writer.

I developed an appetite for reading quite early. Some success at school in book-writing contests in grades one and two also gave me a prod. But I held back. Of course I was barely seven and simply didn't know yet. My love of drawing had taken over. The writing was shelved.

Heartfelt thanks must go to my first grade teacher who thrust me into the spotlight in singing class. This not only encouraged a love to perform, indeed I already had that, but it's where my heart and soul would discover rhythm, beat and verse.

Writing poetry would not come until much later in my love-struck teens. With the lights on, I continued blissfully in the dark.

At senior school, I was drawn to Art and Drama, yet found a desire and challenge in English. A defining moment came with a perfect score on a creative writing essay. I never dreamed I'd satisfy this teacher's literary capacity, let alone get top marks from the hard-faced dragon. Ultimately, she was an extremely fair hard-faced dragon and I respect her for that. From this one experience, I gained a newfound confidence in my whole creative writing ability. I clicked well with the keyboard in typing class and also had a natural flair for shorthand, the translation of arty scribble to words. The writing was on the wall.

Leaving school to become a full-time graphic artist with a sign company, painting and printing words would give me a new slant on creative writing. Along the way, the desire to write poetry made its approach. An unresolved crush on a guy fueled my first love poem. My romantic efforts unfortunately were unrewarded. However this did help to condition me to bare my soul and start sharing different experiences through poetry. My passion had finally found its fledgling wings.

With incentive and motivation to spread myself thinner, I set up a poetry blog. I soon realized this would not give me the feedback or critique I needed so I abandoned that idea and searched the net again. I then came upon my savior in the form of a community based writing website. I was home at last!

I seemed to land on my feet. So with head down, tail up and fingers flat to the keyboard, I didn't look back. I devoured wordplay like there was no tomorrow and wrote about anything and everything right down to mundane fluff like belly button lint. I had no option but to write and when there was no time left to write, I'd somehow squeeze in a little bit more. It was now part of my daily life and the pen had morphed into an acceptable extension of my hand. A poem about my son's feet inspired a series of little poems which evolved into a children's book published at the end of 2011. I also participated in a group anthology with a number of other poets to raise funds for a worthy cause.

I know that I can and want to write, but most of all … *have* to write. For those who truly understand, it's not an obsession, it's simply a requirement. Seriously. Just like breathing. Or talking.

I'm proud to say I am now talking the talk. The endless stream of words shows no sign of fatigue, change in flow or current direction anytime soon.

After all, you *can't* stop a river.

真 Truth

little white lies

美悟笑情力真知友

*old ships*
*pass in the night*
*to pee*
—Fuller


*political jokes*
*are very embarrassing*
*they get elected*
—Stockwell


*short appendages are*
*fodder for women's humor*
*discussed at length*
—Ross

*diversified folks*
*practice civil liberties*
*apple pie slices*
—Campion

*Mother-in-law*
*a lemon doesn't know*
*it's sour*
—Fuller

*I know all about him*
*— he always forgets*
*how I take my coffee*
—Kammer

*constipated and cranky,*
*our uncle Earl visits*
*strained relations*
—Ross

*SUVs idle*
*in hot parking lots—*
*soldiers die*
—Fuller

*the scent of coffee*
*matches the stain*
*on his shirt*
—Funk

*I can relate*
*on many different levels*
*but his picture is crooked*
—Bonnell


*she shoots him daggers*
*he returns a piercing glare*
*double pain windows*
—Judkins


*some children inherit*
*swear gene from both parents*
*family curses*
—Ross

*men at bar*
*tell bawdy tales*
*imbibe and brush*
—Kammer


*little girls dream*
*of kissing their magic prince*
*and find a frog*
—Campion


*we played on words*
*all day in senryu class*
*sat tired*
—Ross

*shoppers*
*sound the charge*
*on Black Friday*
*who's the real turkey?*
—Stockwell

*I'm an open book*
*unfortunately it's blank*
*like my diary*
—Toole

*the dog*
*worships me*
*I don't miss you*
—Fuller

mask factory
she spends all day
making silly faces

Robyn Corum

*I searched the world over*
*to find my Knight*
*in shining armor*
*he turned out to be*
*The Tin Man*
—Toole

*arena's best bull*
*charges blindly*
*through scarlet cape*
*sword ends*
*in his balls*
—Campion

*dope smoker*
*hits paydirt*
*with housewarming*
*most guests*
*give pot plants*
—Ross

*Canyon Wren*
*notes of liquid silver*
*cascade down twilit walls*
*I ask the campers next to me*
*to turn down their TV*
—Fuller

*overworked husband*
*heads off to catch*
*a spot of fishing*
*the one that got away*
*enjoys reel therapy*
—Ross

*talking sense to her*
*was like talking*
*to a brick wall*
*couldn't get through*
*the cracks*
—Toole

## Who am I as a Woman, Writer, and Lover of Life?
by
Susan Campion

What is my present, past and future?

The following poem may provide some important insights:

> *nieces explain*
> *being sandwiched when dancing*
> *might end in shame*

Just like I felt when sandwiched between two young studs while dancing on a crowded floor in the Gas Lamp District, in San Diego, where everyone was under thirty and I was close to sixty, *I don't give a damn.* And, I figure I'm at that stage in my life where I can say that word if I so choose. *I was and am having fun* And, I've not always been able to do that in my life.

I was smart enough to know I was in control at the moment, comfortable between those two studs.  I am who I am and who I've become and that's who I'll be, until I become who I'll be again down the road.

And just who might that be, today?

Let's start with today.

For half an hour this morning, I did the Stations of the Cross while pricked with pins. I also chanted the same Buddhist phrase a hundred times. I had no idea what the words meant and I didn't ask.

Why? Because I trust Dr. Weng, an acupuncturist, one of my teachers and healers, today. Acupuncture, *Quantum Think* and newfound friends have helped make me feel free and create new leaps.

Once, I was a shy little girl, the daughter of a conservative Catholic father, a Captain in the Navy who held great ambitions for me, his eldest child. *I learned about discipline.*

Once, I was a rebellious sixties flower child who birthed a son while unwed and lost him to adoption. *I learned how to love and deal with lost love.*

Once, I was the only child of four who graduated from college and went on to receive a doctoral degree. *I learned to think.*

Once, I had my picture taken with the likes of Bush, Carter, Clinton, and Sandra Day O'Connor. Those framed 8 x 10s now reside on a shelf in the garage. *I learned to forget and be humble. Sometimes, there are still memories.*

Once, I wrote lengthy educational research articles, published with a whole lot of jargonese. *I learned to be succinct.*

Once, I was a feminist who wore tailored pant suits and ties to give keynote speeches.

I liked the style and wear it today, along with my daily comfy sweat pants, sweatshirt, or even jammies and no bra. *I learned to be myself.*

Once, I was told:

"Susan, you will never succeed; you are attractive, sexy, intelligent, smart, and you threaten the hell out of the men who determine your fate."

I never thought of myself that way, never thought life was like that ... *and I learned to rebel.*

Now, I only feel blessed.

In summary, I've reached a point in my life where I can laugh, at myself and all around me.

I observe the world and no longer try to determine what it should be.

*It is what it is*
*and it is what it was,*
*and it is what it will be.*

For sure, I can influence the world with a positive intent, but that is the only influence I attempt today.

I've become a participant in life, enjoying the moment, whether I am sandwiched between two hunks or chanting words even I don't understand.

And I still have that feisty side inside which will always remain.

*she wraps her arms*
*around a downy pillow*
*feathers fly*

I've learned, at least for today, what's important in life.

# A Thick-Skinned Farmer Girl

by
Dana Furrow

I started writing as a young girl: a daily journal/diary, short stories, speeches, and plays. I would cast my brothers and friends to be in my plays, and we would perform them for my parents and their friends at gatherings. I continued writing through high school and a bit in college. In 1991, I married a farmer and began having kids. Sadly, my paper remained blank until three-years ago.

After seventeen years of farming and raising kids, I realized how much I missed writing. In the spring of 2009, I signed up for an online creative writing class through my local community college. I added a grammar refresher course to the mix because it had been so long since I had taken a class or written anything of substance. After a year of writing classes, I joined an online writing site and dove head first into the writing scene.

I learned that writers have to be thick-skinned and resilient. I still find posting my work online terrifying.

I started writing *haiku* when I was struggling with flash fiction. I learned that I was writing contemporary *haiku*, not traditional *haiku*. I signed up for a Japanese short form class to learn the Japanese aesthetic and to do justice to my *haiku*. I took more classes to learn other Japanese forms such as *tanka, haiga, haibun* and *senryu*.

That's when I learned to love *senryu*. Writing all forms of short Japanese poetry has made me a more proficient writer in all my writing. I appreciate the discipline and challenge of these forms.

Writing takes me away from the mundane. It frees me to create and be heard. I love putting my imagination to work in stories and my words in poems. Every day brings new learning as I continue to grow with the women writers who share my passion for words and expression.

知 Wisdom

with thyme comes a sage

美悟笑情力真知友

*a book never opened*
*will never be read*
*and remains a mystery*
—Toole

*just married—*
*he gives up his rights*
*to the closet*
—Furrow

*seeing no need*
*to act her true age*
*she chases rainbows*
—Stern

*I search high and low*
*and cannot find*
*the glasses in my hand*
—Fuller


*kindergarten teacher*
*calls police for assistance*
*child resists a rest*
—Yocom


*he brings me roses*
*after he raises his fist*
*this time too late*
—Chiechi

*we speak*
*of silent stillness*
*and lose it*
—Marshall

*last night's prom balloons*
*reduced to dancing*
*on their own strings*
—Funk

*life...*
*I think I might die*
*before it's over*
—Bonnell

*such an orderly mind*
*I want to dismantle it*
*at any time*
—Creager


*food for thought*
*it's all I ever*
*think about*
—Toole


*before class*
*substitute teacher reads*
*Math for Dummies*
—Furrow

*cornucopias*
*breed boredom*
*less is more*
—Marshall


*put an end*
*to illiteracy problems*
*write for free help*
—Stockwell


*kids tucked in bed*
*and hubby asleep after sex*
*her time to write*
—Chiechi

*maternity floor*
*priest walks out carrying*
*a small bundle*
—Funk


*dreams in black and white*
*stalk me through the night*
*why not Technicolor?*
—Corum


*breath mint kiss*
*I suspected all along*
*he's a smoker*
—Judkins

*angels dance*
*on the head of a pin*
*why can't I?*
—Corum

*an apple a day*
*keeps growers in great riches*
*dentists always win*
—Stern

*at the age of eight*
*granddaughter is fast published*
*time to redo will*
—Creager

*put my two cents in*
*when asked for an opinion*
*never got change*
—Toole


*white-robed altar boy*
*lights seven candles*
*with both soles blinking*
—Funk


*her income*
*is fixed*
*she can't budge it*
—Yocom

*X-ray vision—*
*seeing through my daughter's*
*boyfriend*
—Furrow

*love dances*
*inside every atom*
*divine signature*
—Marshall

*a naked lady*
*sighs in her lilac-scented bath*
*a poem's birthplace*
—Noel

*wisdom waits*
*for me to mature*
*lingering childhood*
—Stockwell


*I'm checking you out*
*with my new library card*
*should be a good read*
—Toole

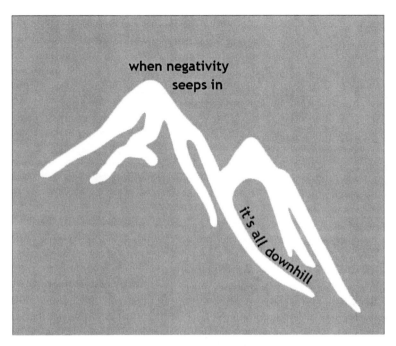

when negativity
seeps in

it's all downhill

**Marie Toole**

*caper bush*
*hugs a Tuscan wall—*
*do you mind*
*if I pickle your buds*
*for my shrimp pasta?*
—Judkins


*my teen son*
*in love*
*requests my advice*
*I rush to comply*
*while still needed*
—Chiechi


*fourth-grade teacher*
*awards spelling prize*
*applause and a hug*
*instructor beams*
*wistful memories*
—Corum

*learning computer skills*
*is difficult for seniors*
*I was just getting*
*the hang of it*
*when my mouse died*
—Toole

*cup of hot tea*
*neglected on the counter*
*gets ice cold*
*a lover overlooked*
*in the hallway*
—Creager

*her recipe file*
*I put dibs*
*on the card*
*that's smudged*
*and faded*
—Funk

*cooking lessons*
*for my son and daughter*
*she learns*
*easy recipes; he learns*
*to flatter her new-found skill*
—Judkins

*getting older*
*has its unique beauty*
*soft and comfy*
*like a worn saggy couch*
*a perfect fit for a weary butt*
—Stockwell

### Fishing and the Art of the Japanese Short Form

by
Vicki Bonnell

I'm somewhere between old and young, sage and dumb, aware and adrift. In short—pardon the pun—I am a student. A student of nature, and the nature of humans, which pretty much covers the waterfront. I'm a fisherwoman, too. That's relevant. See, everything is relevant. That's what I'm just beginning to learn. Everything's relevant.

My ocean of study, my fishin' hole, so to speak, is Japanese Short Form poetry. It's ironic that one so renowned for running off at the mouth should find it so rewarding to eagerly restrict her pen to the confines of anciently structured brevity. Perhaps, but as I say, I've always been a fisherwoman. If the connection between fishing and Short Form poetry isn't clear to you, perhaps you should try to write a *haiku*. A fish won't just jump into the boat, and neither will a *haiku*. That's just the beginning of the similarities.

Speaking of fishing, one of my favorite books is Ernest Hemingway's *The Old Man and the Sea.* You've got your vast ocean. Your huge fish. And, alas, your tiny boat. That's Japanese Short Form poetry in a dinghy. In case you're wondering, the tiny boat represents the finished poem. I'm sure you can figure out the rest. Without challenge, there can be no art.

Maybe you understand what I'm trying to say, or maybe you think I've been out in the sun too long. In any case, I urge you to get yourself a tiny boat. Lord knows, you're already afloat on one grandmother of a sea that's already chock full of more fish than you can shake a Mrs. Paul's at. So smear on a little sunscreen, and let's go fishing. You might be surprised at what you catch.

You know, if Hemingway's Old Man had been a Japanese poet, instead of a Cuban peasant, the sharks might have gone hungry.

See you on the sea – of poetry.

## Life is Good

by

Robyn Corum

I've spent a lot of time trying to figure out what to put in this essay—to give you a real glimpse into who I am, as a writer and a woman. The easy part: I'm the proud mom of three unbelievable children: Melanie, Tanner and Riley, and lucky mom-in-law to Art. I'm an ecstatic wife—married to my dream guy and white knight—and we live in a tiny town in North Alabama. Life is good.

The harder part is giving you an insight into me, and why I write—and why I write *what* I write.

I love kids. I love life. I love waking up to a new day and finding the joys that await me: in nature, in people, in the surprises I come across. I love learning. I love reading. And I *adore* writing. When I was twelve I would climb to the top of our hall closet with my books and magazines and isolate myself from the rest of the world. It was just me in a three and-a half-foot square with a dangling light cord and a bare bulb. It was heaven.

As I've gotten older, my writing seems to take the place of that hall closet—it's where I go, to forget about what bothers me or to examine it in exquisite detail. I write about what I see, and what I wish I could see. I make up characters and then tell them what to do and they do it, unlike in my regular life.

I've been influenced by some of the greatest writers of all times: E.E. Milne, James M. Cain, Margaret Wise Brown, Dr. Seuss, Mark Twain, Robert Frost, Rudyard Kipling, and others. Most of them write with great humor and the joy of discovery, with passion and joie de vivre. I hope that is what the majority of my writings will convey.

I write about serious things: a hurricane in Florida and its aftermath, the death of a cashier. I write about silly things: a blade of grass, a candy zoo.

Recently, I write Japanese poetry. There's a website online that asks you to write a story in six words. To me, this is what Japanese poetry is about: shaving off all the edges and handing the world one small, sharp piece of metal. It can reflect or it can cut. But it does so with a minimum of words and the writing isn't muddied by excess.

I plan to continue creating *senryu*, *kyoka* and *haiga*. If not for the world, then for me, for the little girl in the hall closet, with the door closed and the world shut out.

If you happen to enjoy my writings, that thrills me to no end, and I thank you for taking the journey with me.

*"Words are sacred. They deserve respect. If you get the right ones, in the right order, you can nudge the world a little."*

—Tom Stoppard

## *Senryu* and the Art of Awareness

by

Nina Marshall (Rama Devi)

I consider every aspect of life an art form, the most important being the art of enlightened awareness.

My initiation into the spiritual path commenced at age sixteen, when I simultaneously began to write short creative 'bursts' in my well-loved journal. These insights included inklings of dissatisfaction with society's usual avenues of success. For example, I wrote: "We tend to be so concerned with trying to 'become somebody' that we neglect to be who we are."

This search for the unchanging Self ultimately led me to India, where I've lived with my guru, Amma, for over twenty years. Amma means 'Mother' and she is the embodiment of supreme love and compassion.

About twelve years ago, I offered Amma a poem. She read it attentively and said, "Make a book." Through my poetry, I explore various aspects of her teachings of compassion, patience, humility, surrender and unconditional love—all of which are qualities of the universal feminine archetype.

Amma often says, "You can't write the word honey on a piece of paper and lick it to taste sweetness." You must consume honey to know its taste. Yet to one who has experience, the words can serve as a reminder.

In poetry, often what is subtly scribed into the silent spaces between the words is what has the most impact.

My writing life and spiritual life are deeply intertwined. Through the avenues of reading and writing, my interest in meditation and the spiritual journey first took root. It is through my interest in the irony of expressing the inexpressible that my love for poetry reaches its fruition. Thus, it seems as natural as rain rolling down a mountain that after thirty years on the spiritual path, my muse feels prompted to share insights of this journey through writing. I think the idea of the Zen Satori 'insight flash,' that can be used in *haiku*, can also be incorporated into *senryu* and other Japanese forms. As the tone and tenor of my themes tend to be philosophical and mystical, I enjoy the challenge of producing concentrated works with simplicity, directness, and brevity.

# 友Friendship
### bosom buddies

美悟笑情力真知友

*relatives are*
*the most difficult*
*to relate to*
—Toole

*Grace in the middle*
*of an argument—*
*never met her*
—Bonnell

*Grandma rocks*
*to Sinatra's tunes*
*back and forth*
—Campion

*stand close and smile*
*as if you like each other*
*family portrait*
—Chiechi

*it turns out to be*
*a one-sided conversation*
*he's tone-deaf*
—Toole

*obits*
*faces of the dead*
*smile*
—Funk

*my ex-husband's body*
*under front porch —*
*buried treasure*
—Kammer

*at local cafe*
*women  gather to chat*
*toot toot toot*
—Noel

*she nods approval*
*while I eye candy selection*
*Mother knows best*
—Ross

*hum of the hand vac*
*tabby appears*
*for his sweeping*
—Funk

*rustling in the attic*
*my mind wonders*
*why so early?*
—Bonnell

*it's not what you said*
*it is what you didn't say*
*that I heard you say*
—Toole

*snow melts slowly*
*and leaves drop on ground*
*women share handkerchiefs*
—Creager

*after her service*
*I stare into the portrait*
*we fought over*
—Funk

*a true friend*
*remembers your birthday*
*but forgets your age*
—Toole

facebook—
so many old friends
without a photo

**Carol Judkins**

old couple
sit on park bench
with hands clasped
no need
to converse
—Chiechi

her last
I love you
I hesitate
to erase
my sister's voice
—Funk

ladies' book club
meets to share
good wine and gossip
most forget
their books
—Chiechi

*wrong number*
*we talk*
*for half an hour*
*about being*
*snowed in*
—Funk

*nonstop voices*
*gossip in my head*
*mad tea party*
*of incessant chatters who*
*lie through my teeth*
—Stockwell

*I want to know*
*your past and present*
*'cause I plan on*
*keeping you*
*in my future*
—Toole

## Dancing in the Dark

by
Carol Judkins

At what moment do we call it a flower? Becoming a writer is a process for me, growing and sometimes blossoming, yet deeply rooted now in the fertile soil of Japanese short form poetry.

Working in Public Health for thirty years, I focused on the big, big picture. I think we can't fix our national obesity problem when children are unable to go outside and walk a mile without being shot, for example. I moved from doing district home visits to managing grant programs and Public Health centers to leading the Public Health Nurses in our county as Chief Public Health Nurse. Working as a woman, a nurse, in a man's world certainly required having a sense of humor to disarm and diffuse absurdity. It required diplomacy too—if I said exactly what I was thinking, it would benefit neither my nurses nor the clients they serve. I stopped short of completing my PhD at the dissertation. I was simply too busy trying to make things better in our communities to devote the requisite time a dissertation deserves.

Imagine then, the freedom I felt when I retired two years ago to write what I want to say—but my goal then and now is to do it well.

So why did I choose rule-bound Japanese short forms? As I began my journey, puzzle pieces collected earlier in my life began to fall together effortlessly. I am a long-time student of Eastern religions, deep ecology and metaphysics. I've learned to use breath in meditation. All this together created a deep resonance with the Japanese aesthetic in *haiku* and *tanka*. It taught me to focus, and to observe mindfully. So I set about to learn the rules and write, write, practice, practice. I must tell you, when I got frustrated trying to produce a good *haiku*, I wrote a *senryu*. I still believe it's a very satisfying alternative to Ativan.

I read a lot, too. I began to see lots of variants to the rules in highly regarded journals, and considered all the reasons. I read the debates between traditionalists and those wishing to expand these forms in the English Language. Modern versus traditional—was there any hope of intersection? Could I just willy-nilly swim off into the deep end when I had barely learned to dog paddle? I pondered the possibilities.

Subject matter for satire and irony is endless. I love the challenge of a rant in a minimalist *senryu*. I resisted *kyoka* for a bit, because I love *tanka* so much, but the expansion of acceptable subject matter and tone allows room to poke at human foibles and the human condition in a myriad of ways. I think it helps to study *haiku* and *tanka* before trying to write good *senryu* and *kyoka*, following the modified axiom: "First, know the rules before you expand them."

I think one can enjoy *senryu* and *kyoka* without knowing the ins and outs of the form. I know it works if I see you shake your head up and down, with or without a smile. That nod confirms that it resonated with your experience somehow.

Writing can be lonely work, but women value connection. Whether we are mothers or not, we get older and we care about world issues. We are sexual, we struggle, suffer loss and grief, honor our spiritual selves, and we are fallible, as are the men in our lives. I thrive within a community of women writers who embrace diversity and celebrate differences as we notice the ironies in life, satirize human foibles, and laugh at ourselves. We dance in the shadows, bringing light into the darkness through our poems. These women laugh knowingly at the holes I poke in pretension, and tell me when it didn't work. How can I do lonely work like this without a community of caring cheerleaders?

hugging myself—

I try to remember

the last time I was me

**Dana Furrow**

## Author Bios

### Melissa Bickel

Melissa wasn't born with a silver spoon in her mouth, but her parents and those around her introduced her to the richness and bounty of words. Life for Melissa took many twists and turns, so it wasn't until later in life that she truly experienced the fullness and excitement of writing.

She is a survivor, having gone through a divorce, cancer, and raising a teenager on her own. She's learned what the word humility means and tries to live humbly each and every day. Her successes aren't awe inspiring, but they are successes none-the-less. She's won first prize in a state-funded writing/poetry contest. She's sold a few pieces of poetry and prose on the Internet and writes on many creative sites. Melissa hopes to grow more as a poet.

Until then, she is enjoying a new relationship with a man who's also a writer. Life is starting over at the ripe old age of forty-six for Melissa and she loves it.

Melissa's work has been published in *Prune Juice*.

**Vicki Taylor Bonnell**

Vicki lives in Northern California. She comes from a rich heritage of pioneer families who have left her with stories, books and songs of their journey across the Wild West in the mid-eighteen-hundreds from England. Huntsville, Missouri is named after the fifth of her great grandfathers. They are her heroes. She grew up on ranches in wide open spaces. She loves the wilderness, rivers, streams, lakes and the ocean.

Vicki is a retired interior designer and author of one arts and crafts book called *Let It Dough Let It Dough Let It Dough.*

## Susan Campion

Sue has travelled her entire life, both as a Navy brat and as an executive in the K-12 education non-profit arena. These experiences taught her to embrace diversity, to be strong, and to appreciate stability, friends and home. As a middle school teacher, principal, national consultant and executive in non-profit organizations, Sue worked with challenged young adolescents and teachers in the "toughest" schools in large cities throughout the United States. She led a $13 million contract to coach teachers to believe in the capabilities of all children and hold high expectations. Sue has a doctorate degree from the University of Washington.

Sue learned and practiced the power of self-fulfilling prophecy. Her willingness to break rules and create turnarounds in schools has been documented in multiple books. Her three younger siblings tell tales she no longer wants to hear.

At the ripe age of fifty-seven, Sue met her soul mate and has now been married to her spry seventy-seven year-old John for four years. Her passion is writing poetry and she has been published in three anthologies. She also keeps herself busy with golf, bridge, and reading. Varied life experiences now help Sue move to her next phase of living life fully.

## Connie Chiechi

Connie was born in a small town in central California, where she lived until age twenty, at which time she moved to Sacramento and attended college. She has remained there ever since. She has experienced many great joys in her life: a loving husband and daughter, an extended family, a sweet but neurotic dog, faithful friends, travelling, yoga, bicycling, and writing poetry.

Connie taught college composition for a number of years and loved interacting with young students, helping them improve in their writing. At last, she is retired and can pursue what she has always wanted to do—write.

## Robyn Corum

Robyn lives in Hartselle, Alabama, with her children and husband of twenty years. She takes much of her inspiration from past experiences and leans heavily on a colorful imagination for the rest. She enjoys cooking, crafting, reading, writing, and spending time with her children.

Robyn creates short stories, poems, novels, and most recently, Japanese poetry of all forms. She especially believes in the possibility of happily-ever-after endings.

## Nancy Bravo Creager

Nancy lives in Bremerton, Washington, with her husband and youngest daughter, who is developmentally disabled. She has four children, four grandchildren, and surprise—a set of great grandkids, twin boys, just a year old. She feels blessed. Nancy was born in South America; English is her second language. She loves the challenge of those irregular verbs and double meaning words.

Most of her life, Nancy has been a nurturer. Now in her late sixties, she takes care of herself, and of course, follows her first love: reading and writing. She likes prose and poetry; different forms and styles keep her brain going. One of her autobiographical stories was published in *Chicken Soup for the Soul* and one of her many poems in *Gulf Coast Anthology of Poetry*.

## Alvin Thomas Ethington

Alvin is a displaced Southerner, both in time and place. He learned proper Southern values from his father, the second son of State Senator Peter H. Ethington. He was raised in the Southern diaspora in Casa Grande, Arizona, to an old Southern family and has degrees from Oberlin and Yale. Did he mention he considers himself Southern?

He currently lives in the granola bowl on the left coast of the United States; that's Southern California for the uninitiated. He has published *senryu, haiku*, and *tanka* and writes in English, Spanish, and French.

He is honored to be the only male connected with this project. All his Southern *Steel Magnolia* relatives, both living and dead, told him he had to put that in.

## Suzanne Fuller

Suzanne is a writer, graphic designer, amateur photographer, and a student of animals and nature. She grew up on the beautiful coast of New England, and now lives in Kingston Springs, Tennessee, with her husband of thirty years. She is a graduate of the University of Massachusetts at Amherst, Maryland College of Art and Design, and the Art Institute of Boston.

As a full-time graphic designer for marketing and advertising, she enjoys the problem-solving process of visual communications, and this carries over to her writing as well. For Suzanne, good writing is the successful completion of a puzzle. She has always enjoyed the natural world and has traveled extensively and experienced all types of landscapes. Nature informs much of her work.

She is also a professional horseperson and currently volunteers with an organization that provides the riding experience to handicapped children. Suzanne finds that the incredible bond and understanding that forms between the horse and child is a constant source of inspiration and respect. They find a way to communicate that we can only imagine.

Writing poetry has just recently become a creative outlet for Suzanne and she finds it an endlessly challenging and gratifying exercise.

Suzanne has been published in *Prune Juice*.

## Lois J. Funk

Lois is a widow who enjoyed nearly fifty years of marriage with her husband, Fred. She has traveled extensively outside the U.S. and lived in Australia during her high school years. Her inspiration comes from childhood, sisterhood, womanhood, wifehood, motherhood, and grandma-hood, plus several years of secretarial work, for paying and non-paying "bosses," including her husband and various family members.

She is an internationally published poet and children's author. She also enjoys writing inspirational music, mostly for children. She is a member of several websites that advocate poetry.

## Dana Furrow

Dana grew up in rural Maine, the oldest of three children and the only girl. She now lives and works with her husband of twenty years and their three children on a hazelnut and Christmas tree farm in western Oregon. When she's not tending the family business, she's caring for her horse, sheep, cattle, chickens, and garden.

She spends her precious time trail-running with her border collie, kayaking, biking, reading, skiing, and writing. Her passion is writing young adult stories.

Dana thrives on learning and recently discovered Japanese poetic forms. She has entered her work in flash fiction and poetry contests and has won many. She wrote a short story which she dreams of working into a novel for young adults. Her work has been published in *Prune Juice*.

## Carol Judkins

Carol lives in Carlsbad, California, where she can breathe the sea air. Presently retired from a satisfying career in Public Health, she loves traveling the world with her husband, John.

Carol is a social justice advocate, a romantic, a non-swimmer, a mother, an independent film lover, a perpetual dieter and ancestor hunter—all of which provide inspiration for her writing. Her work has appeared in *Prune Juice*, *Frogpond, Mayfly,* and *Ribbons*.

## Deborah Kammer

Deborah enjoyed her childhood divided between city life in Sydney, Australia, and her grandparents' home in the red soil of the Great Australian Outback in the wheat sheep belt of New South Wales. She was a wife for twenty years, and is now divorced and a single mother of three wonderful sons for most of twenty-three years.

She made a life choice to leave her literature and philosophy studies at University to assist her husband in business. She found her own success in real estate. Life's roller coaster prevented a return to complete her degree, yet led to extensive travel within her own country and overseas, which gave her vast hands-on experience in many fields.

Deborah is an advocate for making changes in the injustice of the status quo and now has the opportunity to embark on a writing career, utilizing her vast field of knowledge and eagerness to learn much more. Her inspiration is her passion for life.

## Rama Devi Nina Marshall

Rama Devi Nina involves herself in diverse creative activities: poet, writer, musician, healer, spiritual counselor, coach and graphic designer. She also works as a freelance editor and writing consultant.

Nina grew up in New York City. She attended Oberlin College and Heartwood Institute of the Healing Arts.

At a young age, she developed a strong interest in spirituality and journeyed to India to pursue a spiritual path under the guidance of her Guru.

For more than two decades, she has dedicated herself to this path and also engaged in extensive volunteer service. Her service activities arc through a variety of avenues. For the past ten years, she serves as a counselor-chaplain for sick and dying patients and their families at Amrita Institute, a super-specialty hospital in India.

Through diverse writing styles, Rama Devi Nina explores theme threads of unconditional love and compassion, spiritual awareness, philosophical pondering, and echoes of the infinite. She considers poetry the music of words and vehicle for expressing the inexpressible.

## Nessie Noel

Born in the 1940s, Nessie grew up on a large, working cattle ranch in Alberta, Canada. At the time, this ranch ran a forty-thousand-cow/calf operation. As the only daughter of loving parents who were survivors of the dirty thirties, Nessie was sandwiched between two rough and tumble brothers. Inevitably, she grew into a tough little tomboy who spent almost all her spare time riding horses.

During the long, sweet summertime of childhood, she was free to ride the dusty trails, mostly alone, exploring the joys and beauty of her rustic and unspoiled surroundings. In these formative years, she forged a lifelong bond with Nature. Although poetry has always danced in Nessie's heart and mind, it was only after her much loved husband passed away that she began to seriously explore it.

Being the mother of six children, three who came into the family through adoption and three who came into it through birth, and being Granny to fourteen grandchildren ranging in age from two to nineteen, this wannabe poetess, has indeed much life experience from which to draw her words and ideas.

In addition, for a number of years, Nessie and an American friend have been developing a geologically based concept, which Nessie first conceived in a dream. This children's project is described at www.Roxplorers.com.

Currently, Nessie is working to complete a book about a playful, adventuresome little rock -as in stone- character. Stay tuned.

## Phillippa Ross

Born in Outback Australia in the late sixties, Phillippa is the youngest of three siblings. She actively pursued creative writing from an early age, and with a love of song lyrics, found an appreciation for meter and rhyme. Phillippa embraced the arts in her academic years and went on to become a graphic designer for two decades. She also owned and ran a sign business for fourteen years with her husband. They have two children. Embracing motherhood and leaving the boardroom, she discovered the joy of writing again. She predominantly pens biographical poetry, incorporating satire, as she loves to laugh.

Since joining a community-based writing website over two years ago, she has been published in a poetry anthology as well as her own series of poems inspired by her children. Her interests other than family include reading, listening to music, drawing, oil painting, airbrushing and scrapbooking.

Phillippa currently juggles a small Internet-based business as well, and will attest that life really does begin at forty.

## Joan E. Stern

Having taught French for seven years, Joan returned to graduate school for a Master's degree in Public Administration. She used it in positions at various universities and the Getty Museum in Los Angeles, California.

She spent the last fifteen years of her professional life as a business consultant. In addition to writing poetry, which has been published in a number of anthologies, and painting in acrylics, she enjoys living in Malibu and delights in traveling.

Joan attends plays, concerts, and museum events with her husband, Bob, who studies the governmental process focusing on strengthening democracy, which sometimes provides further travel opportunities. The other man in her life is their son, Ryan, who keeps her up-to-date regarding technology and popular culture.

## Karyn Stockwell

Karyn, born and raised in Buffalo, New York, moved to Northwest Indiana as a young teenager and remained in the land of cows and corn ever since. While trying to find her identity as a flower child, she changed Karen to Karyn to remind herself to always question the "whys" of life, and because she's different. She also hoped, someday, to write about it in the third person.

She wears many hats, and although some appear off-kilter, she's most proud of her hats labeled registered nurse in the Newborn Intensive Care Unit, mother, Irish, and writer. Her sense of humor and love of laughter is her foundation in life, and Karyn strives to share smiles and positive energy with hopes of making the world a happier place.

Karyn is known to drive with cool shades on, top down, real music blasting, and with her hair blowing in the breeze as visions of Pulitzers dance in her head. Some day, she hopes to own a convertible.

## Marie Toole

Marie is a Brooklyn girl, born and raised in Bay Ridge, and the middle child of three sisters. Presently, she lives in the warm south in Delray Beach, Florida, after retiring from the travel business. She is busy scrapbooking for her six grandkids and loves being in the kitchen, cooking and baking their favorite treats.

Marie is an avid reader and loves writing. It is her passion. Now retired, she has time to pursue what she loves the most.

Marie has been published in *Prune Juice.*

**Sally Yocom**

Music and poetry have been with Sally all of her life. She served as music director for a radio station, where she also performed a piano program every week called *Sally's Magic Fingers*. Can you believe that title? She was music supervisor for two public school districts, and gave private piano lessons for many years.

Now that Sally is retired, she has won several prizes for her music compositions, including one written for a full symphony orchestra. Most of her compositions have been performed for audiences. Her other favorite art form is poetry, and she greatly enjoys writing poems of many different styles, though she especially likes to use wordplay.

As a member of Mensa, she has had at least one poem published in every monthly issue of the *Central Ohio Mensa* magazine for the last nine years. She has twice won a Mensa national award for poetry. Sally's book, *Elements and Styles of Poetry,* is being used in several high schools, which pleases her very much. Life is good.

## Index of Authors' Work

Melissa Bickel

3, 5, 26, 45, 55, 59, 60, 71, 143

Vicki Taylor Bonnell

4, 19, 21, 22, 35, 39, 43, 76, 96, 111, 123, 131, 134, 144

Susan Galletti Campion

i, xi, 53, 61, 63, 94, 97, 100, 102, 131, 145

Connie Chiechi

9, 25, 26, 56, 60, 62, 64, 72, 79, 110, 113, 120, 132, 137, 146

Robyn Corum

4, 19, 42, 55, 58, 71, 73, 74, 81, 99, 114, 115, 120, 125, 147

Nancy Bravo Creager

20, 22, 25, 27, 36, 44, 62, 75, 112, 115, 121, 135, 148

Alvin Thomas Ethington

vii, 149

Suzanne Fuller

xix, xxi, 4, 12, 19, 36, 37,40, 43, 54

93, 94, 95, 98, 101, 110, 150


Lois J. Funk

20, 22, 35, 37, 38, 40, 56, 60, 71, 75, 81, 82, 95,

111, 114, 116, 121, 132, 134, 135, 137, 138, 151


Dana Furrow

3, 6, 10, 21, 23, 56, 58, 72, 75, 80,

105, 109, 112, 117, 142, 152


Carol Judkins

xv, 6, 9, 10, 11, 24, 37, 96, 114, 120, 122, 136, 139, 153


Deborah C. Kammer

3, 5, 6, 54, 57, 62, 66, 76, 94, 97, 133, 154


Nina Marshall (Rama Devi)

21, 23, 74, 76, 80, 111, 113, 117, 127, 155


Nessie Noel

7, 39, 57, 73, 77, 85, 117, 133, 156

**Annotated Bibliography**

SELECTED RESOURCES FOR *SENRYU*

Blyth, R.H. *Senryu: Japanese Satirical Verses.* Hokuseido Press, Tokyo, 1949. Though difficult to locate and out of print, this is a classical resource.

Greve, Gabi. *Haiku, Senryu, Zappai.* Available online at http://haikutopics.blogspot.com/2006/12/senryu-and-haiku.html

Ketchek, Michael, Bob Lucky and Lucas Stensland. *My Favorite Thing.* Bottle Rocks Press, 2011. Reviewed by Liam Wilkinson, former editor of "*Prune Juice*" (November 2011).

Pinckard, William. *Some Senryu About Go* found at: www.kiseido.com/sen.html

Pizzarelli, Alan. *The Serious Side of Senryu.. Simply Haiku,* Vol.4, No. 3, Autumn 2006. Available online at www.simplyhaiku.com/SHv4n3/senryu/senryu.html

http://raysweb.net/senryu/
This site created by Ray Rasmussen contains definitions, discussions and links about *senryu* from a variety of sources.

Reichhold, Jane. *Senryu as a Dirty Word.* Available online at http://www.ahapoetry.com/AHI%20senryu%20art.html

Reichhold, Jane. *Apples, Apples and Haiku.* Available online at www.ahapoetry.com/senarti.htm

Rosenow, Ce. *Written in the Face of Adversity: The Senryu Tradition in America.* Literary Imagination (2010), 12(2), 210-228.

Sato, Hiroaki. *A brief survey of senryu by women.* Modern *Haiku* 34.1, Spring 2003. Available online at www.modernhaiku.org/essays/senryuWomen.html

Takiguchi, Susumu. WHCSENRYU, Volume 5, Issue 1 (2005).

Ueda, Makoto (Editor and Translator). *Light Verse from the Floating World: An Anthology of Premodern Japanese Senryu.* Columbia University Press, 1999. A review of the book by W.H. Higginson is available online at http://2hweb.net/wjhigginson/Reviews/Ueda-Senryu.html

**SELECTED *HAIGA* RESOURCES**

**Please note: Editor or contact information is correct at time of publication**

Addis, Stephen. *A brief history of haiga.* Available online at http://reedscontemporaryhaiga.com/AddissHaigaHistory.htm

Other good interviews, articles about *haiga* and online exhibitions are available at http://reedscontemporaryhaiga.com

**The following selected journals publish *haiga*:**

http://ahundredgourds.haikuhut.com

www.dailyhaiga.org
**Linda M. Pilarski, Editor**

http://www.haigaonline.com
**Linda Papanicolaou, Editor**

http://notesfromthegean.com
**Andy Pomphrey, *haiga* editor**

http://simplyhaiku.theheartofhaiku.com
**Robert D. Wilson and Sasa Vazic, owners**

https://sites.google.com/site/worldhaikureview2/whr/home
**Susumu Takiguchi, Acting Editor**

## SELECTED *KYOKA* RESOURCES

**The following essays discuss *kyoka* as a *tanka* subgenre versus its own genre:**

Garrison, Denis M. *Defining tanka.* Available online at http://themetpress.com/tankacentral/library/research/defining tanka.html

Kei, M. *Kyoka.* Available online at http://kujakupoet.blogspot.com/2006/06/kyoka_06.html

Kei, M. *11 Good Kyoka: Experiments in English.* Modern English *Tanka*, Volume 1, Number 1, Autumn 2006, p. 192. Available online at http://www.scribd.com/doc/18384734/Modern-English-Tanka-1-Autumn2006

McClintock, Michael. *Notes on form, techniques and subject matter in modern English tanka.* Available online at http://tankaonline.com/Notes%20on%20Form%20--%20Michael.htm

**Classic *kyoka* resources:**

www.viewingjapaneseprints.net/sitemap.html
This web site is designed and written by John Firillo. There
is a good exploration of ukiyo-e Japanese art prints. His
topical essays "The *Kyoka* Craze", "What is the Floating
World" and his discussion of Edo artist Isoda Koryusai are a
good introduction to *kyoka* verse prints. Excellent
bibliography throughout the site for exploration in greater
depth and to locate holdings of these prints with *kyoka* verse
in museums.

Gill, Robin D. *Japan's Comic Verse: A Mad in Translation
Reader.* Paraverse press, 2009.
The author requests you check the errata he prepared at
http://paraverse.org

**Journals that specifically publish *senryu* and/or *kyoka*. Please note: Editor or contact information is correct as of publication:**

*Atlas Poetica*. M. Kei, Editor. Available online at
http://atlaspoetica.org

*Prune Juice*: A Journal of *Senryu*, *Kyoka* and *Haiga*. Curtis Dunlap, Editor. Available online at
http://prunejuice.wordpress.com

*World Haiku Review*. *A Journal of the World Haiku Club*. Susumu Takiguchi, Acting Editor. *Senryu* archive available online at
http://wharchives.wordpress.com/2012/03/31/senryu-election

Note: *Senryu* poetry also appears in the pages of many leading *haiku* journals, often unsegregated from *haiku*.

*Frogpond*, the journal of the *Haiku Society of America*, sponsors an annual *senryu* contest. *The Haiku Society of America* website is http://www.hsa-haiku.org

**A sampling of published compilations of English language *senryu* or *kyoka*:**

Kei, M. Catzilla! Keibooks, Perryville, Maryland, 2010.

Rotella, Alexis. *Ouch: Senryu that Bite.* Modern English Tanka Press, Baltimore, MD. 2007. See also her blog at http://alexisrotella.wordpress.com

Stevenson, Richard. *Windfall Apples: Tanka and Kyoka.* March, 2010. Also available at www.scribd/doc/32917452/Windfall-Apples-Stevenson

Welch, Michael Dylan (Ed.). *Fig Newtons: Senryu to Go.* Foster City, California: Press Here, 1993. (First published anthology of English Language senryu).

## Note from the Publisher

It has been a distinct pleasure to work with such a professional and gifted group of poets as those contributing to *Pieces of Her Mind.* As their vision came together and the book took shape, an idea occurred. It was such a unique and unusual book, the reader was bound to want more.

With that in mind, the poets have created a resource of Questions and Answers, Ideas for Discussion, and Potential Assignments to encourage the creation of similar learning communities and expand thinking around the poetic forms and content. This resource will be updated periodically and could be used for groups like college courses and book clubs.

Please visit our information page at
OmegaPublications.net/Pieces_of_Her_Mind_Detail_Page.html
or just click on the book cover at the
Omega Publications Book Store,
OmegaPublications.net/Book_Store.html

CPSIA information can be obtained at www.ICGtesting.com
Printed in the USA
BVOW081336261012

304053BV00001B/2/P